"PLEASE MISS"

A.C. Griffiths

ARTHUR H. STOCKWELL LTD.
Elms Court   Ilfracombe
Devon

ISBN 0 7223 2176-7

Printed in Great Britain by
Arthur H. Stockwell Ltd.
Elms Court   Ilfracombe
Devon

CONTENTS

"PLEASE MISS"

"I want to be a nurse," I stated with what must have been boring regularity, when, as a child I worshipped at the hem of my Red Cross aunt's starched apron; but like the voice crying in the wilderness I was unheeded if not unheard, and a teacher I became. Not, I may add, because of a particular brilliance on my part, but because I had a very determined headmistress whose idea of heaven was Edge Hill (or some other college), and somehow I found myself (still protesting but with less and less hope of success) going in for one examination after another like one in a trance.

Having survived an excellent but extremely chilly college in the north of England, the next thing was where to teach. Again under protest (I seemed to spend my time protesting without any success), I was appointed to a school outside Manchester in a very poor — and what proved to be — wonderful neighbourhood. Little did I think, as I walked up to St. Gabriel's on a day (April 1st above all days!) in 1930, that I should spend fourteen very happy years there with the best staff, the finest headmaster, and the greatest lot of children one could wish for.

Until that day "Those Dark Satanic Mills" had been something we sang about. True I had wakened from childhood within sound of the clatter of 'clogs' taking their owners to work at six o'clock in the morning, but on that day I literally walked between those mills, along a canyon of road — truly the "valley of the shadow", the mills were so high — graced by the name of Grimshaw Lane. Grim, yes, but lane! Once perhaps. Now it was paved with grey stone 'sets' and with large 'flags' as paving stones for a footpath. As one passed an open mill door, a blast of hot oil-laden air hit one, and there was cotton everywhere. The very air seemed full of it.

On that day began some of the happiest years of my life. All years are a "mixed bag", but friendliness and humour and kindness make even the grimmest surroundings in their way beautiful in memory. "Never judge a sausage by its skin", my aunt used to say, and that might sum up the school. The building, when I reached it, stood on a piece of "spare ground", with a croft on one side and a playground with a surface like a nutmeg grater on the other. It had in front of it a low brick wall, old as the building itself.

Eyed by several very interested — what would t'new teacher be like? — young people, I entered timidly. Passing a tiny hole of a cloakroom on the left, and the Infants' Room on the right, I went straight on through the only doorway left, and turning a heavy iron ring in a very solid door, I entered a long room — the hall, if it got its right name. Usually referred to as the 'all because this was Lancashire at its best.

The 'all turned out to be three class-rooms divided from each other by screens. The headmaster occupied the "centre pitch", and a young man and myself had the spaces left on each side. A tall 'Scrooge-like' desk graced the head's position. We, if we sat down at all, sat with the children. I have often wondered how they managed to sit as still as they did on those hard benches.

In my first year of teaching I "grew up" considerably. Not that I considered myself specially naive to start with, but this was a tough district, and when the headmaster said "Oh well, what can you expect when his grandfather is his father?" I must admit that I went back to my class-room and thought about it, with a startling result! The boy in question could neither read nor write, but his colour sense was terrific. He used colour with joyful abandon and effect: deep rich colours which blended into a striking beauty. This love of colour and art was general in the school. The children, living in a drab district, took joyously to art as young ducklings take to water.

There being three classes in one room presented some problems of course, but also, as a bonus, a good deal of entertainment at times. It was the custom in those days for ''Dinner-Takers'' to be allowed out of school early to take the dinners to those of the family who worked in the mills. Each day, the door used to fly open regularly at ten minutes to twelve and a voice reminiscent of the Flying Scot going through a small station, called ''Cec-il!'' Reminiscent too, in that when the outer door opened, any loose papers that might be lying on the desks took flight like the newspapers from a W. H. Smith's bookstall.

Our 'Air Raid System' was sufficient without the help of Cecil's mother, for it went off with great effect when there was no need, and kept silent when there was.

Cecil, by the way, had earned himself among his companions for obvious reasons, the name of ''Gaupus''. For no apparent reason, except that they ''felt like it'', when we were at camp in Derbyshire they tossed him up in a blanket. When we appeared on the scene he was flying up and down quite happily.

We camped on one occasion at a place called Disley, outside Manchester, and not far from Buxton. The camp was 'run' by a very kind farmer whom the children immediately nicknamed ''Strawberry-Nose''. I have no idea what his real name was.

The site was a sloping one, and the tents had wooden floor-boards. There was only one camp bed — a sort of truckle bed, which collapsed on the slightest provocation. This was much coveted though in spite of its disconcerting habits, because when it rained the water ran *under* the bed instead of through it! There were eight staff with the party, four men and four women. We ladies slept feet to the middle, and to we younger ones it was great fun; especially one night when a great hairy head pushed itself into the flap and gave a companionable "moo". We hadn't taken much notice that there were cows in the field during the daytime, but we got quite used to hearing in the night heavy breathing very close to one's head, which was of course near the side of the tent.

How the men fared *we* didn't know until one night we caught Jimmy, whose hips were too thin for those floor-boards, blowing up his mother's air-ring. I believe he stepped into this as if about to take to the water, before he lay down hopefully to rest. It was Jimmy also who ate a piece of laxative chocolate in mistake for a piece of Rowntrees. As the loo — such as it was — was situated away in the far corner of the field, it was, as you can imagine like an obstacle race against time, falling over startled cows en route.

In the evenings, so as not to be too much kept in, we took turns at going *out*, and one night for a bet the hair-pin-like Jimmy undertook to crawl the length of a new sewer pipe they were laying on the main road. Were we frightened! Jimmy was such a nice chap and we longed to see him again. It seemed an eternity before he emerged, grimy but triumphant at the other end.

On one occasion in "The Big Room" as the hall was called, it was a Composition lesson following a Hygiene lecture on the 'Common Cold', which was prevalent at the time. "Coughs and sneezes spread diseases" we wrote. All was quiet except for the scratching of the old-fashioned pens, and the odd sniff. When suddenly, rising like a cartoon balloon from the ranks came an indignant voice — "Don't blow yer breath on me!"

Composition lessons often provided some gems of learning. On examining one little girl's composition on "Someone I know" I read "My auntie has various veins".

Anyway, I had said "Tell me anything!"

One dull day in November, feeling rather the worse for wear after a period with 3B, I sat down to mark some Composition books. "An Adventure I Once Had" was the title hopefully suggested as giving the imagination a chance to flourish. The first book opened cheered me in spite of myself. It said "How I was eaten by a Canniball"; whilst a further effort by one of the girls concluded "An exciting ship-wreck", "Then I was rescued by a sailor and raped in a blanket".

Misnomers too provided some hilarity when exam time came round. It was only when you read "Judas Iskaricot" that you realised you had missed out somewhere. A Karricot was very much better known to them than Judas all those years ago, and if under a picture of a giraffe it confidently stated "This is a girootle", who am I to blame? After all it's the thought that counts!

It is not surprising that some names stick in the mind. There was Arthur Wright, who at once became "Rheumatism" of course. "Brittle Bones", whose real name I cannot now recall. His bones broke with little or no reason. Then there was "Sonny", the texture of whose skin led one to suppose that he had been dug up like a potato, rather than born in the normal way. Oddly enough, his head, close-cropped, was not unlike a potato in shape. A nicer, cleaner family, never lived. It was just the way he looked. His brother provided me with the classic answer of all time in Lancashire. Asked to write the word "comfort" into a sentence, he wrote in the most perfect script — "Landlord comfort rent". Eddie Bowden was another interesting scrap of humanity. Hard and bullet headed with steel-rimmed glasses on a small thin pale face, he looked tough, but tough in a nice sort of way like a little old man.

On my first pay day — which comes eventually, even though there does always seem to be more month than money — I had promised to take my mother to tea at

Parker's in Manchester and on to a film afterwards. Parker's stood in St. Ann's Square, and was the height of my ambition then as treats went.

The afternoon, a Friday, arrived and so far all was well. It was the last lesson, always a favourite because it was "Story Time". I sat perched somewhat precariously on top of the front desk, my feet on the seat. This, besides being a good vantage point was the only available seat as we were now in what was called "the little room". Toad of Toad Hall was keeping his audience enthralled as usual, and we were all relaxed and happy. A storm raged without, but what of it? With Toad for company and who knew what joys ahead over the weekend?

Suddenly — Wham! One of the top "hopper" windows was blown open, glass splintering in all directions. So surprised and startled were we that for a moment no one said anything. Then Eddie put up his hand to his bullet head, and it came away RED! "Bludd!" he shouted in pure Lancashire, and then continued to yell with horror!

The door shot open and in came the headmaster to see what all the noise was about. Luckily it was only a minor cut. Eddie's head, though protected only by a "crew cut" was tough, and the doctor's not far away. I got him there with the assurance before we set off that he was "a tough guy" wasn't he? He agreed, and stopped sniffing on the promise that a model yacht which had been used in a drawing lesson, should be his on our return.

It was this same child who caused quite a stir in psychological circles — unnecessarily, as we pointed out at the time.

Eddie had "Free Dinners", and on Fridays it was fish, and when every Friday came Eddie was adamant: he couldn't eat fish. At the Centre where the meals were served to these poor little charity scraps of humanity, they said he was "a) Stupid, b) Defiant, c) Mental, and must be sent away."

The doctor wanted to send him to a psychologist. We

said "Ridiculous and quite unnecessary. Eddie isn't mental, there must be a reason for it." So the headmaster, a very humane and understanding person, said "Let's see what he will tell us on our own." The meeting was arranged at a suitably private moment in "the little room" (the head had no study, the school was so poor), just the three of us, to see if mutual trust could do what authority could not. And it worked!

"Now", said the kindly headmaster, "you can tell your teacher and you can tell me why you really and truly cannot eat your fish on Fridays. You need not be afraid. We won't let anyone punish you or take you away."

"Well", said Eddie, "it were codfish."

I felt that the vital truth was very near. "And you don't like codfish?" said the head kindly. "I'm not very fond of it myself."

"No," said Eddie, "it weren't that! Ah were full o' tatas!"

THE WAR

Being uncomfortably near A. V. Roe's (the munitions factory) we came in for more than our share of attention from the German Air Force during the war. On one occasion I was alighting from a bus on the opposite side of the road to the school, when I looked up into the face of a German pilot. We were so near that at the time I didn't realize it, and we passed each other on our own separate ways quite calmly.

These were what we called "Nuisance Raids", and were timed to coincide with the neighbourhood's dinner time break. Almost every day, promptly at twelve o'clock the sirens would go, and we went across the croft to the air raid shelters near the playing fields, quite a little distance from the school.

On one such hurried expedition one middle-aged member of the staff was seen to be hurrying back across the open ground to the school building. "Never mind your register" shouted the head, "leave it!" (I might mention that the register was a "must" in case of a direct hit.) The figure, however, scurried on and later returned.

"Whatever possessed you?" said the usually patient headmaster. Better lose your register than your head."

"Oh it wasn't that," came the reply, "I was worried about catching cold. I had forgotten to put my hat on."

At this same school we had an infants' headmistress

who was a real character, and also a very thorough teacher. She prided herself that reading was her strong point and did everything to encourage it. Miss Swain was her name but the infants invariably spoke of Miss Wain. It was her custom to give , every now and again, a number of books as prizes for reading, books incidentally which were samples left by travelling salesmen. On one such prize giving occasion, a shocked murmur went up at one point from the assembled ranks, and a horrified gasp.

"Miss Wain," piped up a strident voice, "she sweared!"

"Oh I'm sure you're mistaken," said the diplomatic headmistress consolingly, looking at the accused, a neat little girl with brown ringlets bobbing.

"No, Miss Wain" chorused several other witnesses, "she did. We heard her."

Thinking to keep the affair as quiet as possible Miss Wain called out one dependable child and said, "Suppose you come and whisper, and just tell me what you *think* she said."

The whisper came "I've seen the bugger before!"

Being a Church School we went to church on such days as Ash Wednesday and Ascension Day. Pilate very often became "Contius" instead of Pontius, but we sang with great gusto, our lunches — those who had them — discreetly out of sight under the pew. We were in the middle of "All things bright and beautiful", and the sun shone through the stained glass windows on to a peaceful charming scene, the daffodils and primroses with which the church was decorated, scenting the air. Suddenly, came a jarring human note. An irate young voice piped up "He's eaten mi lunch!" We obviously had an opportunist in our ranks.

THE NEW TEACHER

"She's strict, but boy, can she draw!" was Alan Ketts' summing up of yours truly after a few days as his form mistress. This was typical of the attitude of most of the children; they took you as you were, good and bad, and accepted discipline if fairly dealt.

There is a terrific feeling of 'one-ness' in a class such as my first class at St. Sampson's enjoyed. As at St. Gabriel's they were a 'C' stream, and as such not wanted by many teachers. They also shewed a ready response to art in all subjects. One boy, a big blond youth with large slow blue eyes, had a particular wish to shine. If any country or place was mentioned, he claimed to have a relative who lived there. This, his companions quickly spotted and enjoyed. One day when I announced that we were "visiting Africa today", the whole class with glee chorused — "Miss, Ward's auntie lives there!" and rolled about in their desks with mirth. I laughed with them enjoying the feeling of good humour and comradeship.

On one occasion, when all was quiet, one child slipped out to me and smiling, put a finger to his lips, nodding towards Ward's desk. There he lay, his large blond head on his arms, sound asleep. I shook my head and said "Sh!" and with conspiratorial glee we waited for Ward to waken up and complete our enjoyment. He did eventually of course, amid hoots of laughter, not a whit perturbed by their mirth.

Someone in later years said he came back to school and claimed, when asked what he did for a living, that he drove the Flying Scot! Heaven help the passengers if *this* one of his myths was true.

Children can be very cruel to each other sometimes, without meaning to be. One day, all the class was waiting to set off for church for the Carol Service, always a popular and enjoyable affair, and I had given a 'pep talk' before dinner as to what preparations should be made for visiting God's house in the afternoon.

I made a great point of the fact that you need not feel at all embarrassed if you had no *new* clothes to wear. That didn't matter. But you should be clean and tidy and look as nice as you possibly could with what you had.

We were all assembled, shoes, hands, and face inspected for cleanliness when the door opened, and in came a very nice plain child, who always tried to please. She had obviously made a great effort. Her clothes were her "Sunday best", and although her hair was straight as a lath, it had been brushed well, and her plain, well-groomed head was surmounted with an enormous bow.

Without any hesitation, as with one voice, that class gave a spontaneous cry — "Easter egg!" Sure enough that's what she did remind one of, but I could have strangled the lot of them. The poor child was in tears, but they guffawed happily, until I put my spoke in. I pointed out that an Easter egg is a very nice thing to be — a very special thing, dressed up for a special occasion. I also added, for good measure, that she looked a good deal better than most of them. This brought complete silence, and they marched off, chastened, I hope.

GOING TO THORNHAM

Migrating to a little country school from this large town one, was a complete change. When the time came for me to leave and a presentation to be made in front of the whole school, one tall gangly boy in short pants would persist in putting up his hand. He was waved down repeatedly by the head, who was becoming more and more annoyed at the interruption. Thinking eventually that it might be good policy to listen, he said "Well, what do you want?"

"Please Sir," said the boy, "is she coming back when she's better?"

One even asked if I was going away because I didn't like them any more. Those children were poor but they were a grand lot.

You reached Thornham School with its tiny "Mickey Mouse" bell-tower on top, by climbing a stony hill with hawthorn hedges on either side, and a toll gate (no longer in use) half-way up the lane. Larks sang, and there was a feeling of quietness and peace as you entered by the front door, which had originally been the main door of the little church. The one-time vicarage stood next door in an old world garden, and fields stretched away as far as the eye could see. A far call this from St. Gabriel's and the "dark Satanic Mills".

Most of the children were from the surrounding farms, the rest, the village children. When the snow was deep, one

mother quite cheerfully cut a way to school for her little
girl with a fire shovel!

Again there was the one big room, but how different!
The windows were unstained glass church windows with
side low stone sills. At one end, where the altar had
originally been, stood the head's desk on a platform which
overlooked the senior class.

My juniors occupied the rest of the room, the infants
being completely separated from us by a wooden partition.
They had an old-fashioned coal fire with a fire-guard. The
vestry was now the kitchen. A delightful place and
delightful country children with very co-operative parents.
Quite different in many ways, but nonetheless the same in
some respects, as the school I had just left.

Here life was gentler and the children reflected the
difference. One father, a farmer, would appear every so
often and "round" up his little family — some with deep
red-gold hair, some with black shining locks, but all curly-
headed — and take them to the barber. There was a
friendly atmosphere of co-operation and understanding.

The even tenor of our ways was broken at times of
course, as when young Thomas (not 'Tom' or 'Tommy'
please!), and his little brother ate the family cheese ration
(war was still 'on'), and then fell into the ship canal and
drowned. Thomas was a tiny child — a kind of Tiny Tim
— who wore inordinately large boots; and when the day
for the funeral came we, much against our better instincts,
were bidden to take the infants down to line the lane
leading down to the little country church as it was the
mother's wish.

The infants' teacher being absent, I was given charge of
this group, and having lined them up, bidding silence, took
up my place at the lych gate from where I would view the
ranks as it were. Imagine my horror, when, as the funeral
cortège came in sight, a welcoming shout went up —
"Hurray! Here's Thomas!" In life as in death, Thomas, in
his man-sized boots, was just as dear to them. On a similar

occasion when I was "standing in" for the infants' teacher another embarrassing situation arose.

It was the visit of George VI, then King of England, and his Queen to open a new luxury ballroom and public swimming bath in the town. We were taken down by bus and given priority of place on the front row because of the shortness of our legs.

The royal car was late in arriving. We wriggled impatiently after the first few minutes' wait, and then, the outriders were sighted, at last! All eyes were glued on the royal couple — with complete interest. At least, I thought so, until, looking along the line I saw one small boy smiling broadly, his face almost hidden by the large buttered muffin he was eating!

OLD JACK

Old Jack Boswell lived in a gypsy caravan not far across the field from school, on a piece of land lent by a kindly farmer. His sole companions were a cat and a few hens, and his caravan like himself was always spotlessly clean. He was liked and respected by everyone, and the children never referred to him as Old Jack or Gypsy Jack, but always, with great respect "Mr Boswell".

Old Jack — he didn't know his age — was small and neat and brown and clean, with always a spotless 'kerchief tied round his skinny throat below his short, well-kept beard, neat like the rest of him. The children loved him and were very kind to him, ready to help if he should have need of them.

The only time really was when he had a letter from his sister, his only living relative who could write. He would bring the letter to the school door, sure of a welcome always, but not wanting to intrude, and one of the children, delighted and proud to be of service (and to have the ability!) would read it to him. If the words were sometimes pronounced a little oddly, Old Jack drank them in avidly with the rest, a happy, satisfied smile on his thin face, and then retreated with many thanks looking as if he now really belonged to somebody! It was very pleasant to see the two heads bent close together, one young and the other old, peering at the letter with enthusiasm, quite natural and both happy, each in their own individual way.

Brenda Tomlinson was usually the favoured "Reader". Brenda was a farmer's daughter and a dear soul — if the term can be applied to a twelve-year-old. Her enthusiasm and co-operation knew no bounds, and at Christmas time when the party loomed large in everyone's mind, Brenda's contribution was a trifle. And what a trifle! Huge in a glass bowl, at least four inches deep in thick farm cream. Well, the cow itself would have been proud of it! It added some confusion to our Nature Rambles (there was plenty of nature to ramble in round Thornham) when it came to naming the various flowers we found.

"What is this one?" I asked hopefully, holding up a Bird's-foot Trefoil.

"Bird's-foot Trifle!" piped up Brenda with a smile, happy to be on familiar ground.

WHEN THE BEES CAME TO THORNHAM

That was the day! or rather, the morning. It was Sunday and, warned by our enthusiastic headmaster to dress suitably for the occasion, we came. A strange and motley assembly gathered in the lane awaited our arrival with the colony which was coming by train from Hereford in a special travelling box. The head met the bees at London Road Station, Manchester.

Outfits varied, striped pyjamas tied round the ankle with string predominating. All wore brimmed hats with veils, some black, some white, to protect the face. This added a sinister and macabre look to the scene. Elastic bands at the wrists completed the outfit. Surely no bee could intrude past these ramparts, but you'd be surprised!

THE SWARM

We place our faith in a book called "Digges", which told you what to do in any emergency. Digges, I believe, was a clergyman and was irreverently referred to because of his likeness to one pallid member of our Bee Club, as "Coffin-nails".

"In the event of the bees swarming", said the book, "and you do not know from which hive the swarm has emerged, take a small quantity of flour and sprinkle this gently on the bees. In this way you can identify them."

Someone was hurriedly despatched to the nearby school house, which had once been The Vicarage, and returned with a 2 lb. bag of self-raising flour. We, in our ignorance, sprinkled assiduously, and all was going according to plan when it began to rain! A nice steady drizzle, enough to set those bees frothing and staggering round as if inebriated. They really "bumbled"!

On another occasion the bees chased the gardener (bees hate the smell of corduroy trousers) all round the garden and down the lane. One afternoon — warm and sunny and ideal for the trip — they decided to leave home for higher places, taking up residence, their queen safely in their midst — on a tall sycamore tree nearby. What fun! The headmaster, who fortunately had served in the navy and was used to giddy heights, had to take a skep up to fetch them. When tea-time came, more fun! The bees showed no signs of settling in the skep, and we on the ground decided that this was thirsty work.

"What about me?" came an irate voice from above; so by devious devices his tea was sent up. It involved a basket and a rope — so we all brought our chairs out to watch from a safe distance.

In spite of — or perhaps because of — these extra activities, we got better results than any school around.

We kept bees at St. Sampson's also for some time, until I was stung so badly on the legs that they both swelled up and resembled bolsters, and frightened the headmaster so much that he insisted on me seeing a doctor. If I was going to die I mustn't do it in school time! I explained that if I had been going I should have departed this life within the first few minutes of being stung. The doctor, by the way, informed me that I should have lain down immediately and kept still. As the hives were situated, though he didn't know it, in the midst of a bed of nettles, I took rather a dim view of this advice!

Once, on Sports Day, they clouded gaily across the centre of the field and settled in the school nurse's garden ; and another day chose the edge of a quarry on a ledge about twenty-five feet up, whither yours truly had to climb to retrieve them, having borrowed a nearby builder's ladder. The headmaster and deputy head gave me support by holding the foot of the ladder! Eventually when the bees had to go, we gave them away, (one should never 'sell' bees) transporting them in a van with the hive shutters closed; but not closed enough. One by one those bees crept out, and we had to open the van window to let them trickle their own way out, shedding bees, one at a time the whole length of the island. Next morning when we got back to the school garden most of the colony must have returned! Why ride when one can fly?

MRS MILLS AND CLIFFORD

At Thornham our allowance of milk (one-third of a pint each in those days) was delivered to school by Clifford, who was Mrs Mills' husband. His arrival each morning was heralded by the front door opening and a mighty "crash!" as he put the metal crate down. "Gummy", he would say laconically and sometimes added more in an equally unintelligible fashion, mainly because his teeth would not allow anything nearer the truth.

"Good morning Mr Mills," I would carol gaily and then quietly to Margaret Fitton. "What does Mr Mills say Margaret?"

She was a born interpreter and never failed me. "He says there's some short, but he'll come up again," she would say matter of factly.

"Oh thank you!" I would call and everybody was quite happy.

One day we were walking down Thornham Lane, a pleasant enough walk if a bit hard on the feet, when Mrs Mills pulled up alongside in the milk-float, drawn by the same old brown horse that snorted at Jack Wood in the rounders' match, and frightened him into such unaccustomed activity.

"Jump in!" called Mrs Mills cheerily; her rosy face alight with good humour. "Riding's better nor walkin' any day."

In this case it was doubtful. A milk-*float,* as you know if you have lived long enough, was balanced on two wheels; wheels hard-shod with a rim of iron, and with a step at the back for mounting purposes. I climbed in, Jack ("the Boss") followed, but at that particular moment the old brown horse decided he'd had enough. Mrs Mills' weight on the back step proved too much, and if it hadn't been for her brawny arm and a hand like a huge ham, we should have all been deposited on the flint road. One clap on Jack's back from that mighty hand and he almost shot over the horse's head in front! For Mrs Mills with her curly brown hair and bonny figure had some weight behind her.

It didn't always avail though, as on the night just before Christmas when they had poultry thieves. Thinking to be "on to a good thing" they bought an old Manchester Corporation double-decker bus and had it installed in the field near the farmhouse. Here the poultry were to be housed. Cliff was a slight pale man, the reverse of his wife, and Cliff liked his sleep.

"Cliff!" hissed his spouse in a meaningful voice, "get up!"

"Hu?" replied Cliff.

"Get up! Burglars," said Mrs Mills with even more force.

"Hu?" replied Cliff. "Where?"

"In't th'enhouse," came the reply

"Then thee goo and see to 'em," said Cliff reasonably, "they're your hens, so they're your burglars."

VETERINARY ASSISTANT

Teachers do not only teach. They have other interests. I love animals but never had a chance to work with a vet until during the war years; they started animal clinics where people who could not afford to go to a vet, could come once a week free. The vet, of course, was paid.

It was in this way I got my chance. With other ladies of the town I sat and took down names and addresses as the animals were brought in.

One night my chance came, the vet came to the surgery door and said "Can anyone come and help me tonight as I'm on my own."

I stood up and said "Yes, I will."

He said "Will you be sick or faint?"

I assured him that I would do neither, and in I went.

I had no qualifications of course but I did have the very responsible job of watching the animal (mostly cats), and if it stopped breathing during the operation I was to tell the vet immediately. It only happened once — and it was saved. The vet held it firmly by the back legs and swung it through the air to get the air into its lungs. I watched with great faith, until at last the vet told me to call its owner, an old lady, in. By that time the cat was lying on the table perfectly all right.

It was soon after this that I learnt that you can deliver things other than letters. My role then was to keep the cow's tail out of the vet's way! A humble kind of job but very nice when you saw the new calf. Only once one was dead, and I cried. The vet was very kind. He lent me his hanky to dry my tears, took me to a country inn nearby, bought me a drink and took me home.

I wore a white overall to keep my clothes clean, and dear old ladies whispered intimate details about their pets. I had to very hurriedly assure them that they were talking to the wrong person!

It was to this vet that I rang one day in great distress. I had a lovely Red Setter who needed lots of exercise, so if the weather permitted I took her to school with me as this was the little country school, way up in the fields at Thornham.

All day she would stay quietly in my class-room, and when the school dinners were over, enjoy anything that was left.

On this particular day we had walked up the hill through the fields and the wood as usual. But — later I had to referee a rounders' match in a nearby field. The fields stretched far and wide in every direction for we were indeed "Far from the madding crowd". While writing down the score on my pad, I looked up and horror of horrors there was my beloved Setter off over the brow of the hill with Jimmie, the farm dog, on business bent! I had brought her out a week too soon. Somehow I finished the match and sent the children home, then went straight to phone the vet and tell him what had happened. He was a very kind young man with a delightful Scottish accent. I could hear him laughing to himself. I pointed out that I didn't think it at all funny and could he do anything about it.

"Yes" he said he could. "Take her home as usual and I'll come right down."

He came and gave her an injection and I smiled again as I thanked him.

"So that's all right" I said.

"Yes" he replied "but ye'll no have to take her to school again for a further three weeks."

My heart sank, but then I thought anyhow this would be better than seven or eight little Jimmies!

THE VILLAGE SHOP

The village shop was kept by Miss Johnson, a lady of ample means and proportions. She invariably wore a faded mid-navy blue blouse made of poplin, and fastened by two large pearl buttons. Her outfit, during the week never varied, though she must have had an ample supply of these identical blouses as she was always clean and neat and tidy. Her hair was done up in an haphazard bun, and her legs, seen only on Sundays, when she emerged from behind the counter and went to church.

Nearby was a field of autumn crocus. Where they originally came from nobody knew, but they grew on a piece of waste ground as if heaven itself had dropped them there. We feasted our eyes on them in the daytime and prolonged the joy by picking and taking home a few for further delight at home.

Speaking of Miss Johnson reminds me that the only time I ever rode in a police car escorted by a helmeted outrider was when somebody's bees swarmed in a nursery school garden near Rochdale, and had, of course, to be removed with all possible speed. The police rang to ask us to oblige, so it was a case of "If thou wilt, choose me" and off I went, delighted with the ride and a change from arithmetic.

Down the lane we went and out onto the main Rochdale Road, passing Miss Johnson's shop en route. Just to tease her, we didn't call on our way home from school and enlighten her as to why I had been 'in custody'. Next morning we could hold out on her no longer; her curiosity *must* be assuaged.

"Hey!" she began at once, "did I see Mrs G. go past in a POLICE car yesterday?"

"Oh yes," I replied nonchalantly. "Of course I knew they'd catch up with me sometime."

She looked at the head's face, then at mine, and we all began to smile. The irony of it was that I had the ride for nothing. The rightful owner of the bees had come with all speed to claim them before we got there. "A swarm of bees in June . . ." etc.! A good thing really as, apart from my veil hurriedly snatched on leaving, I had no protection but a thin cotton dress and wore no stockings, and only a pair of canvas plimsols. It reminded me that the doctor had already said "If badly stung *lie down wherever you are* and keep still."

When I left Thornham seven years later, the whole school (all ninety-two of them!) came down the lane to wave me off. They cried, with all sincerity, "If you don't like Guernsey come back to us." Happy, kindly, Thornham; with Mrs Whatmough in her mob-cap serving school dinners; along with motherly Mrs Hartley. Immaculate in her white apron and cap, Mrs Whatmough wielded her ladle with determination and persuasion, and was an entertainment in herself.

"I don't like carrots Mrs W."

"Get away with ye, they'll make ye see further."

"I don't want any cabbage Mrs W. It makes me feel sick."

"Nonsense! It'll put skin on your back like velvet. Eat it up!"

St. John's Thornham, was not without its characters, of course. There was Jack Wood, a local farmer's son, who swallowed his prune stones (all fifteen of them), because following a lecture on "Manners when eating" by the well meaning young headmaster, he dare not spit them out! But Jack lived on far less perturbed by the event than we were! Jack had huge china-blue eyes, in a neat, round, fair face; a nice child who rarely spoke and who moved very slowly.

One day, when all the juniors were out on "the big field" playing rounders, Jack was stationed away out almost on the horizon, where he could stand with little or no risk of being damaged by a too fast ball. We all saw the big gentle cart-horse which usually drew the farm milk-float, approaching Jack from the rear, while Jack stood quite unconscious. The whole field waited expectantly. The old horse lumbered on contentedly, until up to Jack's shoulder, and then neighed in a friendly greeting. Jack never ran so fast. The rest of the players rolled about with mirth as Jack disappeared over the skyline.

Then there was the time when in the Christmas play the Knave of Hearts, taking his part too seriously, actually (undercover of the table-cloth), ate the tarts. This was not discovered until an irate Queen of Hearts shrieked in angry tones "He's *eaten* them!"

Yes life was pleasant at Thornham, but time moves on and sometimes we have to move with it. It was so with me. What do you feel when on leaving a child says "Don't you like us any more?" I leave you to imagine.

And now for my next move.

c

TONSILECTOMY

"A doctor? Ooh no, I'm only a teacher."

After I had been at St. Gabriel's, Middleton junction for fourteen very happy years, a doctor decreed that I must move to a cleaner area as I had had tonsilitis four times in one year, and my tonsils were now septic and must be removed. The next thing was to find a hospital which would have me. Rochdale couldn't, because although near, I wasn't in their area. Manchester said the same. I wouldn't go to Oldham in whose area Middleton did come; so our good family doctor said "Never mind, we will find a hospital in Cheshire. I have a friend" he said "with whom I trained, I will ask him if he will do it for me." So he phoned and came back delighted "Old Smithy says he will do it. He's a big man" he said "and he looks like a butcher. He is a butcher but he's a very good one."

So an appointment was made for me to see Mr Smith the surgeon the next day at two o'clock in Manchester at his consulting room.

"Mind" said the doctor, "there are two Mr Smiths in rooms opposite. Don't go to the wrong one; his brother, he's a gynaecologist."

I selected the right door and tapped timidly. No answer, so I walked in to find a large desk as big as a table, a big chair behind it, and a small one in front. This I presumed was for me so I sat on it and waited. Not for long. In came

34

Mr Smith, and he certainly was a big man, but very pleasant. He sat down on his chair and I waited for him to speak.

"Are you a doctor?" he said.

I gasped "Ooh no," I said, "I'm only a teacher."

"Only a teacher?" the big man said smiling. "Well, let's have a look at your tonsils. Yes" he said "those need to come out as soon as possible." (I shouldn't have been surprised if he had said "now"). But no. He said "I will take them out on one condition. You must not teach for a month. Before that you can whisper. Be at St. Ann's Hostel at eight o'clock tomorrow night, and I'll take them out after dinner."

A nice thought! But I said "Thank you" and went.

It is surprising how difficult it is to whisper, but to swallow was impossible. I shed tears into my ice-cream because I wanted it so, but no, I had to wait.

When I eventually went home, of course, our doctor immediately wanted to look in my mouth. "Beautiful!" he said as he gazed at Mr Smith's handiwork admiringly.

A few days later I received a letter summoning me to the jury at Boldon Assizes.

"What use shall I be if I can only whisper?" I said.

"Write it down" he replied. I was still as weak as a fourpenny rabbit, but he said "The only reason for being excused jury service was if you were pregnant!"

Anyway I went, and was glad that I did, it was so entertaining. There were two courts in session at once. I was lucky, I got the smash and grab raid one, the other was very boring, just motoring offences.

The counsel for the defence was brilliantly clever, and played with words like a cat playing with a mouse, having the court in ripples of laughter throughout. When the prisoner was asked what he did in a certain time, he said, "Shall we just say you 'dilly-dallied' on the way?"

The prisoner agreed "Well" he went on to say, "there was a girl. What would you have done milord?"

We went to dinner with the policemen as we weren't allowed out. That was fun for me as I live alone.

At last came the summing up. We said "Guilty, but not proven," and the policemen told us just how stupid we were. The man pretended to be simple and got much laughter from the court, as he would keep addressing the clerk of the court as "milord". In the summing up there were twenty minutes unaccounted for. When asked what he did in that time the prisoner said, "Well, what would you have done, milord?"

That same year I flew for the first time — to Guernsey where I subsequently came to live.

GUERNSEY

A far call from Middleton Junction, or for that matter Thornham, but children are children wherever they live, and the children of Guernsey were more lucky than most in that they lived on a beautiful island.

Approaching Guernsey from the sea one sees a charming 'Pied Piper Town' rising from the waves. From the air the impression is of an island set in a green-blue sea, with a lacy edging of foam around the coastline. Creamy waves break in summer over granite rocks, and in winter when the wind is high, hurl themselves with such violence that spray falls in breath-taking showers of green glass beauty. Cascades of almost ethereal loveliness fall in foam on the darkened rocks, and hiss back to be caught up again. Gulls soar effortlessly in the clear air. Here and there the sun winks and twinkles on the glasshouses with which Guernsey abounds; for tomatoes and flowers are her two main exports.

My arrival the first time was by air. This was when I came on holiday with a friend. We arrived very early on a perfect summer's morning. I had never flown before and felt that I had never been so near to heaven as up in that blue sky, above clouds shot through with the sun's first rays.

I fell in love with Guernsey at first sight. From the moment of setting foot on the island I felt welcome, and safe. It was this feeling and the sheer natural beauty of the place that held me, and made me decide to move from the North where I had been born.

Three years later I came back to teach, and to make my new home here. This time I came by mail boat from Weymouth, armed with a permit to buy or build; and with my teaching appointment safely assured.

My aunt, a dear soul, waved us off, my mother and me, from London Road Station, Manchester, handing us for sustenance on the journey, above all things a large pork pie and a bottle of port wine! Two more potentially bilious things with which to start a channel crossing I cannot imagine.

Everyone was very helpful. The taxi-driver who ferried us across London to the boat-train, quite willingly allowed me to take my dog, a large Red Setter, for a walk in some suitable gardens; and we had a cabin booked on the *Saint Patrick,* my favourite ship, now long out of service.

The crossing was uneventful. We were up on deck early to find the Guernsey waterfront rising on our right, as we passed the island of Herm on our left.

It was into St. Peter Port harbour that we sailed at 5.30 a.m. on a glorious day in August; for I was to take up my new teaching post at the beginning of the autumn term.

We had with us four large suitcases containing our clothing. The household goods and chattels had set sail days previously as freight, and were due to arrive any day.

Actually they arrived most inopportunely as the term had already begun. At 6 a.m. the agent rang to say he was coming to take me down to the White Rock (the harbour), as it was necessary for me to see the containers unlocked, and identify my belongings before they went into store. We had, at this time, only holiday accommodation. If the goods are left to stand on the quay, demurrage is charged for each day they remain; so it pays one to go down and get them moved as quickly as possible.

All went merrily. We arrived at the White Rock, after a

very pleasant ride. It was strange to see the old familiar bits and pieces of home again. Like meeting old friends.

The goods then set off in two containers for storage. We had to follow them, the estate agent and I. Whither I knew not, but it was a perfect morning and still early. Plenty of time before nine o'clock I thought gaily. Arrived at the place of storage, however, which turned out to be the disused stables of a nunnery, we found that only one container had arrived. The other had apparently, taken the wrong turning in the Guernsey lanes. We waited. Breakfast time passed by with an empty feeling within. Still no sign of the second container. I phoned the guest-house to explain that I wouldn't be in to breakfast. Time passed. Nuns walked past and smiled at us. At last, feeling uneasy about my prolonged absence from school (by this time it was past nine o'clock), I sought the telephone once more.

"Where was I?" they asked.

"I don't know which part of the island," I replied, "but I'm in a monastery garden."

So, with the arrival of container number two, began my first day at school. How did I feel as I walked up the broad drive into the park on which the school was set? Very much the same as on my first day of teaching, but this time I was on a headland looking out to sea towards the island of Herm, and I smelled sea air, not oil.

My one fear was that I should not be able to find a suitable place to live, and one that I could afford. Actually I almost did just that, a few days after arrival, but missed it, and had to begin the search again.

Very near though, as if in consolation, a piece of land came up for auction; the very piece on which my bungalow now stands. I bought the land. Now to find a builder.

"No trouble at all," said the school caretaker. "I know just the man you need."

And he did; a master builder, who with his son, a genuine craftsman, made our new home for us. I called dear old Mr Hamon our "Father Christmas", because each time he came to see us he brought us something to please us. A piece of "pop-bottle" glass for the oak front door his son had made, a special kind of tile, which was just what I wanted. He made it easy, and within twelve months we were home! I called it 'Le Souris' because whenever I think of home I smile with a nice warm feeling inside me.

'Le Souris' is, to say the least, homely. When the cuckoo clock, bought to celebrate "Equal Pay", points to twelve and strikes three, it is probably half-past four. It has never been the same since it fell off the wall during last year's spring-cleaning. Several 'operations' have been performed but none with lasting success. The electric clock in the lounge is still half an hour fast, though I retired seven years ago. This is a relic of the time, when, as a teacher I had a horror of being late.

The plastic barrel which bears the words "DOG BISCUITS" has never contained anything but sugar, the tin that says "SUGAR" holds rice, but why worry? This is Guernsey. *We* know, and we live here. Visitors are charmed and soon learn to adapt. They even come again!

But 'Le Souris' is not quite so cuckoo as it sounds.

It is five o'clock on a January afternoon as I write, and from where I am sitting in the lounge by an old-fashioned log fire, I can see the full moon shining through the bare branches of the apple tree. The town church strikes the hour below in St. Peter Port, and the sound is carried upwards on the still air. If the bungalow had grown taller we should have been able to see the sea, for we live on top of a hill, but just a little inland. It is not until one has walked a little way down the road that the sea becomes visible away below, and in the near distance the island of Herm, its well-known Shell Beach gleaming white as the light catches it. A blackbird is singing, "putting the garden to sleep" as we say, and the little camelia bush beside the pillar at the front door is laden with buds, some of them already opening. Soon the magnolia in the centre of the little front garden will be a joy in the sun by day, and then the moon makes it a thing of beauty at night.

To walk down into town from where I live is to feel free for a while from care, happy in the sunshine and fresh air. St. Peter Port, our one and only town is a friendly place of higgledy-piggledy buildings and cobbled streets; streets that climb between the buildings with leisurely gentleness. To see the mail boat sliding in and out of harbour is a very usual sight as you drop the last hundred yards to the waterfront. Slow and majestic she glides past the little island of Herm, one of the smaller and most charmingly beautiful of all the Channel Islands.

The school to which I had been appointed is situated on the headland at the northern end of the island, so it was necessary for me to drive right along the coast road, which was very pleasant. What a change from those "Dark Satanic Mills" days! But the children, and the staff here were very similar to those I had left, both at the town and country schools. They were great. In the staff, I a stranger, found ten ready-made friends, and the children with their enthusiasm for art and general friendliness reminded me very much of those I had left.

There was humour here too. Letters to teacher were often well worth rereading. One in particular springs to mind. It was from an irate mother after a visit from the school nurse. *"Dear Miss,"* it began — unlike one I received which began:
"Dear Sir or Madam.

Your nurse as comes to school sent me a letter today saying as how my son smelt. Well, she must be an old maid if she doesn't know what a man smells like. He only smells same as his father.

Yours

Mrs . . ."

The nurse in question was middle-aged and married, and greatly amused. She saw the full insult of this remark. To be married — smell or no smell — was a mark of success in this part of the world!

One letter I received from father instead of mum. It read — *"You sent the attendance officer to ask why our Mavis didn't come to school and I said she had a boil. He came and wanted to see it, but I wasn't going to let him. It was you know where.*

> *Signed:*
> *Ex-Sergeant Major E . . ."*

One that explains itself if you knew the size of the family, was as follows:

"When they told you our Irene was away from school because I was ill, you asked what was the matter with me. By this time you should know. It's always the same thing.

> *Yours*
> *Mrs M."*

The shortest and most touching letter of all though, came not to me, but to a friend of mine in England. It was from an immigrant mother who, in spite of her large family insisted on calling herself "Miss". She explained this by saying that where she came from they didn't bother with things like that!

It was during the time of "School Dinners", and the trouble was that with all of her children she never had enough money to pay for more than two or three. This was tolerated with some kindness and some necessary explanations by the headmistress. The mother promised to do her best although she said "Business was bad", so the next Monday morning was awaited with interest and some sympathy. The eldest of the five brought a scrap of paper and some Green Shield Stamps in a tattered envelope. The note said *"Sent in good faith"*.

From a friend of mine also comes the anecdote about the Chinese menu card. My friend taught needlework, and when one of her senior classes had finished the dresses etc. that they were making, she suggested that it would be nice to put a little embroidery on them. One that was particulary effective was what looked like a string of

Chinese letters (as it turned out actually to be), going from the shoulder down the front left hand side of the dress.

Intrigued by this, my friend said "Now that is very nice, where did you get the letters from?"

"Off a Chinese menu," came the reply.

"Do you know what it means?" was the next question.

This was answered by giggles and some covert glances among the other pupils.

"We asked", they said, "it means 'This is a cheap but tasty dish'."

REPORTS

Reports too brought in their fair share of hilarity, though not intentionally so. An air of concentration always permeated the staff room when reports were being prepared. What to say about whom? Brows were furrowed. How to vary the remarks?

On one such occasion, the Divinity Master decided there was nothing much else he could say in his final remarks as form master to one of the fourth year girls. She was due to leave anyway, so he wrote "I wish her all the best in her after life." This was bad enough, but worse was to follow. It turned out the girl wasn't leaving!

The parents also had a chance to express their opinion, in a final space headed "Parent's Remarks".

Form master's remarks: 'Your daughter is very trying.'
Parents' remark: 'Yes, she always does her best.'

Religious Instruction Test:
Question: Describe a NUN.
Answer: A virgin in confinement.

Form master's note on passing report to headmaster:
      'An original conception.'
Headmaster, on returning report:
      'No doubt a clerical error.'

The headmaster in one school liked to hand over each report personally for the child to take home. The class was a senior one with a not too bright mental average. The envelopes of course were destined for home. They seldom got so far. On this afternoon a dark solid-looking girl at the back of the room turned to her friend, and after a lot of twittering and whispering, put up her hand, "Please Sir", she asked indignantly, "what does it mean when it says I'm 'a mixed bag'?" On examination, the remark in question had been, "Mary's work is a very mixed bag!"

A subtle and careful way of saying what was difficult to say was "He could but improve". This proved puzzling and on the whole quite effective.

BOY LOST

In the fullness of time it became necessary because of expanding numbers to move some of the children down to the old Church School. There was just room for two classes, so off we went to Potters' Corner. I had a telephone in my room so as to keep in touch with the main school. This of course, had to be on a party line, so one morning, one of my children having failed to come to school, and all efforts to trace him having failed, I tried to phone the police with little success. Two mothers, free for the time being of their duties were having a conversation. I tried for some time to stop them talking but to no avail. At last I jiggled the receiver up and down so violently that one voice said "I think somebody is trying to break in on our conversation."

"Yes I am" I said. "Will you *please* clear the line as I want to phone the police. A child is lost. I am speaking from St. Sampson's School."

The conversation ceased. I waited more patiently now having great faith in the power of the police, until eventually a call came. Someone had seen a young boy heading along the main road for town. He was clutching in his hand a small plant pot decorated with pieces of coloured china and shells. We had made them in class and he was determined that his mother, who had been taken to hospital, should have it. The Princess Elizabeth Hospital was a long way away, but not too far for a small boy to go when his heart was set on getting there. The police, as usual, completed the expedition satisfactorily and then brought the boy back to school.

THE CAROL SERVICE

At one school in which I taught, the music master — a good looking young fellow — became on Xmas Eve afternoon, the organist for the School Carol Service, which was incidentally attended by many of the local people and looked forward to by everyone.

On one such day the organist to be, appeared at school looking very ill with flu. We begged him to go home and go back to bed, but *"no"* he said, this service was eagerly awaited and he would play the organ or die in the attempt. Our pleas were of no avail, but he returned from a visit to the cloakroom and said he was ready. Off we went "in crocodile" as usual. When we arrived at the church he was already seated on the small wooden stool high in the organ loft. Below were the choir stalls, and I couldn't help thinking what a fall he would have, if he fell.

But no! Music began to flow effortlessly from his fingers. I was carried away on wings of sound. We passed from one carol to another, some well known, some less familiar. It was wonderful. The familiar world seemed to have passed away completely for the time being. At last it was over. We were back in the little church by the sea where St. Sampson was said to have landed when he first came to the Channel Islands.

Back at school we asked our erstwhile organist what he was going to do now. "Drink the other half of this bottle" he said going to his locker, "and go straight home to bed!"

48

A TEACHER'S CHILDHOOD

Even teachers have to be children once, and I was no exception of course.

I was an only child with very caring parents and had a very happy childhood, and was, I think with one exception, a good child. The exception was when I almost drowned my cousin Tony, who was on holiday with us. I was a sturdy four-year-old and he had committed what to me was an unforgivable sin — he had broken my doll "Dinah" which he had been forbidden to touch. When they found us we were on the very edge of a mill pond, he face down against the water and me, solid and indignant sitting on his back. Another minute and it would have been too late. I was quite unrepentant: he had been told not to touch my doll "Dinah" (who incidentally was "christened" in a pudding basin!): the teacher in me not liking disobedience?

I loved flowers and filled glass jars with even the most humble. But one day I saw a water-lily at its beautiful best, in the middle of a (fortunately!) shallow lake. The lake was covered with duckweed and I suppose looked to my eager eyes, quite solid. I stepped out to reach the beautiful flower and down I went — in my white needlework dress! I was soon rescued and restored dripping to my dear patient mother.

Another time I was missing, and my over-anxious father was just going to fetch the police when I walked calmly down the road. "You might have known" I said, "if Edie Bamford's cat had had kittens, where I should be." I loved kittens. Our Irish 'Doctor Paddy' hated them. When he thought I was going to die with diphtheria, and said I could have anything I wanted, I at once said "A kitten!" That kitten slept under my chin and I am sure saved my life with its warmth and comfort.

COLLEGE DAYS

Before one teaches one has to be taught, so, before reaching the giddy height of standing in front of a class, fully fledged and come-what-may as it were, came college! To me a cold memory of often lumpy porridge — for the porridge depended entirely on whether the Scottish cook was with us — and "cork-mat" for breakfast, and 'Moby Dick' on a large platter for dinner on Fridays — in an oak panelled dining-room which promised better things! This memory was shot with brief intervals of warm and heavenly bliss further south at half-terms and holidays, when one could eat what one fancied at home, and roast yourself in front of a coal fire.

It wasn't all bad though. In most respects unlike college today, lights went out at 10 p.m. and the doors were locked. Many is the time I have been caught up to my neck in bath water with no idea where I left the towel, or anything else. In time this became a carefully planned strategic operation, with one eye on the clock before you took the plunge.

Then came the surreptitious journey back to one's own room, along dark corridors. Have you, in the black-out, ever put out your hand expecting to feel a wall and encountered fingers on exactly the same errand? The first time, new to the game, I gave a startled squeak, and a low and cultured voice hissed "Be quiet you fool, you'll have us both in trouble.'' I recognised the voice as that of one of our young tutors who occupied the enviable position of the only room which had a French window, and thence access to freedom if wanted.

I had the very doubtful fortune to share a room with a very nice girl, one Edith Twitchett by name. Edith was alarmingly thin and looked anything but athletic, but she had the most deadly stroke at badminton, which dropped the feather, after an apparently long distance flight, suddenly and unexpectedly *just* on your side of the net. The feather appeared to suddenly give up in mid-air and plummet to earth like a stone — always too near the net to reach, but not near enough to touch it. Yours truly was commandeered to practise with her: not because I was any good against the college champion, but every champion has to have a loser and I was an easy victim. The only time you could be sure of getting the use of the gym was 6.30 — 7.30 a.m., as breakfast was at 8 a.m.; so then it had to be. A jolly little activity on a cold morning, but after a while enthusiasm stirred up my circulation for it was a game I enjoyed, and after two years with Edith I became quite good and could almost play in my sleep.

SCHOOL PRACTICE

"School Practice" was part of college, and took place once or twice a year, usually avoiding the winter months. It proved a welcome, if sometimes an alarming change. To be confronted by anything up to a class of fifty, as there were in poorer schools in those days, was a hair-raising experience.

What to do with fifty staring, some giggling individuals, for how many hours before one could escape? 9 a.m. — 12 noon, 1.30 — 4 p.m. Oh well, here goes! Now what did I prepare last night?

In order that we should get as much experience as possible in different types of schools, one "School Practice" was in a very poor district, one in quite the reverse. We were selected to go out and work in pairs — another good idea — for a week. Those in the country areas were taken by special bus, and given a packet of "pond-weed" sandwiches for sustenance until their return.

The first school to which I was apportioned with a very capable student called Eva, was in a very notorious part of the town. Eva was as full of confidence as I was lacking, so it was a good choice on the tutor's part. We were warned never to travel alone in this district, as it was quite a usual occurrence to see a man chasing his wife (or perhaps someone else's) with a carving knife or similar implement. It was whispered that murder had been committed there, but that may have just been a little embroidery put on the actual facts.

Eva and I went in gaily, young and undismayed, with our carefully prepared talk of tadpoles to enlighten the town dwellers "how the other half lived". The tadpoles, needless to say, soon came to an untimely end. We found them one morning floating in a murky sea of lemonade crystals, and the cleaner left because, later, when she went to clean the cloakroom, three frogs goggled at her from under the sink. Talk about St. Trinian's.

One of our tutors, a dear, gentle soul who went by the name of "Woofie", and wore raffia hats trimmed with flowers, got peppered with peas from several expert pea-shooters, and beat a hasty retreat, never to be seen there again.

To compensate, I think, for our 'baptism of fear', Eva and I were next sent to a Girls' Central School. A very different kettle of fish this.

This was a 'pond-weed' sandwich outing, and I was to take French, on my own. To speak a word of English during the lesson was forbidden, and this doesn't half cramp one's style! Mercifully the books were illustrated, and it was obvious that the lesson was about snow and ice and slipping and sliding etc. As there was no spare class-room for us, we had to use the cookery room. There amid the pepper and salt and sugar we sat, my French with its Lancashire accent not making things much clearer. Simple enough I thought, but from the blank looks on their faces I might have been speaking Hindustani. Finally in desperation I took up a piece of chalk and went to the blackboard and drew there-on a sledge, and said brightly but impatiently "Oh! — Comme ça!" A smile lit up their placid faces and hope dawned in my mind.

"Ah oui Mademoiselle" they chorused and I continued to draw, and write the names one at a time. The bell went and the lesson was over.

Our French tutor was a dear old character, a real

gentlewoman. She worked with us so enthusiastically that by the end of the first year, the class which began with fifteen had dwindled to eight, and later ended with four of us taking our Final Oral Examination with Mamselle down on her knees praying for us in the library next door! This, or the fact that there was a gardener at work outside the window with a very noisy lawn mower, probably made for my success, as my answers must have been even more incoherent in French than usual under the circumstances.

On St. Patrick's Day, Mamselle wore a bunch of shamrock skewered with a steel hat pin into her hat, always balanced uncertainly on a bird's nest of hair. She was very quick to take offence and when Isabel caught sight of the shamrock and shewed her surprise in her dark eyes Mamselle burst out in a fury, "You, you *laugh* at me Mees Hurrst!" I was sorry for her because she was so poor and so sincere in her efforts to make us work hard.

On one occasion, I forgot my French exercise, and as French sessions took place in the evenings before supper, it was too late that night to ask me to go out; particularly into the rather dubious district where she had her dingy lodgings. I had to go next morning between breakfast at 8 a.m. and lectures at 9 a.m., and it was at the other side of the town. Up a steep flight of stone steps between bay windows with lace curtains I went and knocked timidly, although she was never angry with me. When she asked me to step inside, there was another flight of stairs, this time wooden ones and sparsely carpeted. She seemed so pleased to see me and I wished she could have known that we really liked her, and not been so lonely.

I always attributed my success in finals to the fact that they took place in hot weather. In winter, once even the ink froze and we were given the day off to go to Middleton in Teesdale and see High Force Falls frozen in mid-air. I can still, in my mind, see the woods carpeted with what must have been thousands of plump snowdrops. Never have I seen more beautiful a sight, and one, like Wordsworth's daffodils, to be remembered for always.

The problem of taking specimens into school for a lesson was that they had to be either collected in the chill light of dawn, or the night before and kept safe until the bus came next morning to collect us and our impedimenta. Worms were easy, if you like picking up slimy things at crack of dawn from the compost heap, but mice or caterpillars were a different matter.

One specimen to each child was the rule, but on one occasion Margaret left the lid of the box slightly ajar, and we were picking caterpillars from the folds of the curtains for days. We lived, twenty-four of us, in what had been a big private house; and the bigger rooms were divided into two or four by curtains so as to give privacy. So those caterpillars had an extensive and happy hunting ground in which to climb, not to mention the bedclothes of course. In college it was a different matter. There they slept in long rows of cubicles with a corridor running down the middle.

One night the specimen mice got out and mingled happily with the usual mouse population. We were studying heredity at the time, and it was a case of "one black, one white, and one khaki" when they'd finished.

I had a very embarrassing experience with my worm in the laboratory. We were studying them in preparation for a lesson, stroking the bristles under them to prove how they moved forward, etc. This always called forth squeals of horror from the little girls in class, though we as biology students had to go horribly further sometimes. On this particular day I put my worm — a fine specimen whom I christened Algernon, in the laboratory sink in the bench in front of me, and turned to listen to the tutor ("Biology Tommy" as opposed to "Little Tommy" another Miss Thomas). Alas I had forgotten to put the plug in and my Algernon had gone, literally "down the plug hole"!

The most difficult school in which we found to teach was a private one situated in the college grounds as a 'Practising School'. There the children arrived either chauffeur-driven or driven by Mamma, and they knew *everything!*

My lesson was on tea. I swotted this up the night before, and coffee also, just for luck. Cocoa never entered my head, probably because I never drank it if I could help it. When the subject was announced they carolled in a happy chorus, "We know all about tea."

"Oh, good!" said I, not to be outdone, "then we'll talk about coffee."

"We know all about that too," they triumphantly cried.

I felt desperate and I did not love my pupils in the very least. Then I had an idea. "Oh good!" said I equally complacent now. "So you can tell me all about them both and I will sit back and listen."

I got the best criticism I ever had for my 'presence of mind', which only goes to shew!

Weekends came, and at the end of the day we slid into our ice-cold slippery sheets. Never were sheets so enthusiastically polished! They positively shone. There they waited on a Saturday morning ready to put on the bed, and if you didn't tuck them in tightly at the foot of the bed, you stood a good chance of sliding straight out again at the bottom.

The people of the North were very kind indeed, especially to we "Southerners" who had no friends or relatives there. There were three of us from Manchester and one (my senior) from London; the rest were "Geordies" and Tynesiders. One half-term I was invited by my junior to stay at her home in Newcastle — which I never saw. We had six feet of snow, the real stuff, and our holiday was notable for the fact that we couldn't get back to college without much delay. *And* when we did eventually travel we actually met some men students, similarly marooned! Unheard of mixing of the sexes in our day at college. To round off the day when we arrived we were allowed a fire in the common room, and cups of hot cocoa at eleven o'clock at night. Such debaucherie!

"EXAMS"

Far from being the dreaded ordeals they are supposed to be today, our children seemed to take them in their stride. When asked what a "temperate" climate was, one boy said confidently "It's 'alf an' 'alf Sir."

Of course there had to be competition to get into Grammar Schools. At Thornham, our three nearest were Bury, Manchester and Middleton and these had to be first sat for, and then followed an oral test if you merited it. As young Margaret Fitton said to her mother as they came down the school steps after the first one, "Well! that's that! Where do we go next?"

On one occasion so great was the interest in the examination results that when one of the school managers died, and the school flag was flown at half mast; one of the infants was heard to say to another, "Oh look the flag's only half-way up. What does that mean?"

"Oh", came the reply, knowingly and quite seriously. "Didn't you know? David Finney is half in Manchester Grammar School."

Talking of examinations reminds me of medical examinations. These too had their moments. At one time we had a very handsome young Irishman for our school medical officer. Came the day when mums were called to attend, and their children's health seen to.

It came the turn of a big bonny lass, forward for her age.

58

She stood and waited. "All right Rosie," said the doctor, busily washing his hands, "take off your blouse."

"What!?" came the startled reply.

"Take off your blouse please," repeated the doctor, turning to face her.

She gave him a coy look and a playful back-handed push. "Oh go on ye cheeky thing!" she cried.

On another occasion, also in Lancashire, the doctor said to the mother, "Take off her vest please."

"Ee!" came the reply. "What a shame, ah'd just stitched her up for t'winter an' all."

I was marking my register one day when a small figure appeared in the doorway.

"He's gone," said the boy as he entered the class-room.

"Who has gone?" I asked, puzzled.

"Mi gran'father," replied the lad. "He's jed."

"Do you mean that your grandfather has died?" I asked

"Aye" said the lad. "He were reading t' "Fur an' feather" (a magazine), and he just warted o'er (fell over)."

The children get to know one very well, and were quick to learn how much I loved animals. My kitten, Tigger, wandered into school one day and was welcomed warmly. To our delight he was not owned, so, after eating part of my luncheon sandwiches and drinking some of the children's milk (very willingly given), I took him home wrapped in my headscarf. He was a diminutive ball of stripy fascination, and lived happily until he was fourteen; much loved by us all.

The story would not be complete without mention of my dogs either, for as some children do not realize, teachers have a life and interests of their own, and it is good to share them.

My first dog was adopted because she was left to fend for herself on what she could catch. Owned by people who were not unkind, but just didn't think that an animal needs kindness and companionship, just like a person and extra food; especially when she is carrying puppies, be they invited or uninvited. This, I think, was a very valuable lesson for the children to learn. That particular dog was fed on their affection, and the remains of school dinners chiefly, and after that would come and lie down in the class-room with the children when it was story-time. She came home with me eventually, with the owners' permission, without a backward glance. It was a great joy both to myself and to the children.

I always had a Red Setter. Mick (who sailed to Guernsey with us), was succeeded by Kerry her daughter who lived to be twelve years old. Then came Tulip. I went to fetch her as a puppy from Derbyshire, and the children were very interested when she went to a show because I took her to school with me in my Mini as the show hall was very near, and I was at work of course. Her handler came soon afterwards and picked her up. All the children wanted to give her their lunch! She would have been in the sausage-dog class if I hadn't kept a sharp look out.

In time — fourteen years later — Tulip and I had to part, and I had another Setter from the same place. One little girl particularly fond of animals herself, brought her a collar — a diminutive sweet little thing that would have fitted a Chihuahua! That same child went after school and every Saturday morning to clean stables out for nothing, just to be with the donkey and get the occasional ride.

On one occasion I took the class to see "Doctor Dolittle" at the cinema in St. Peter Port. We had been reading the book and this was a long promised treat. When we were coming out, the child came to me and gave such a happy smile. "You enjoyed that too didn't you Miss! — I *know* you did!"

But in Guernsey, England, wherever; children are children, and very much the same — just young people. So, in towns, in the country, by the sea; they travel on through life. When a fine strapping young fellow greets you these days and solicitously enquires how you are, one realizes that to him you are a real person, and not just "teacher" any more. Heart-warming indeed I think to know that we've travelled together at least part of the way down the 'Corridor of Time'.